A a

Ideal notebook for preschool children's freehand writing practice

This Notebook Belongs To

_____

EB Creations
Copyright © 2021 by EB Creations Al rights reserved

Aa Aa Aa Aa Aa
Tt Tt Tt Tt Tt
Pp Pp Hh
Pp Pp Pp Pp Pp Pp Pp
Hh
Hh Hh Hh Hh Hh Hh
Pp Pp Pp Pp Pp Pp
Pat Hat

10/5/23

Cat Cat Cat Cat Cat

Pat

Hat Cc

tap tapp tap tap

at	it	ap	an
① Bat	Bit	Map	Man
② Cat	fit	lap	Nan
③ fat	hit	Nap	Pan

in	ag	am	ad
① Win	Bag	Cam	Dad
② Ein	Sag	Bam	Has
③ Bin	Hag	Sam	Lad

NOUN

Person
Place
Thing

VERB

action

Kallan is sleeping at home.

Misha is my running partner.

Teachers are talking at school.

The restaurant is showing a movie

Kalan 8/25/24

it him is sip fit pin pan an nap cat rich spin and find for just many one she then

it him is sip fit pin pan an nap cat rich spin and find for just many one she then

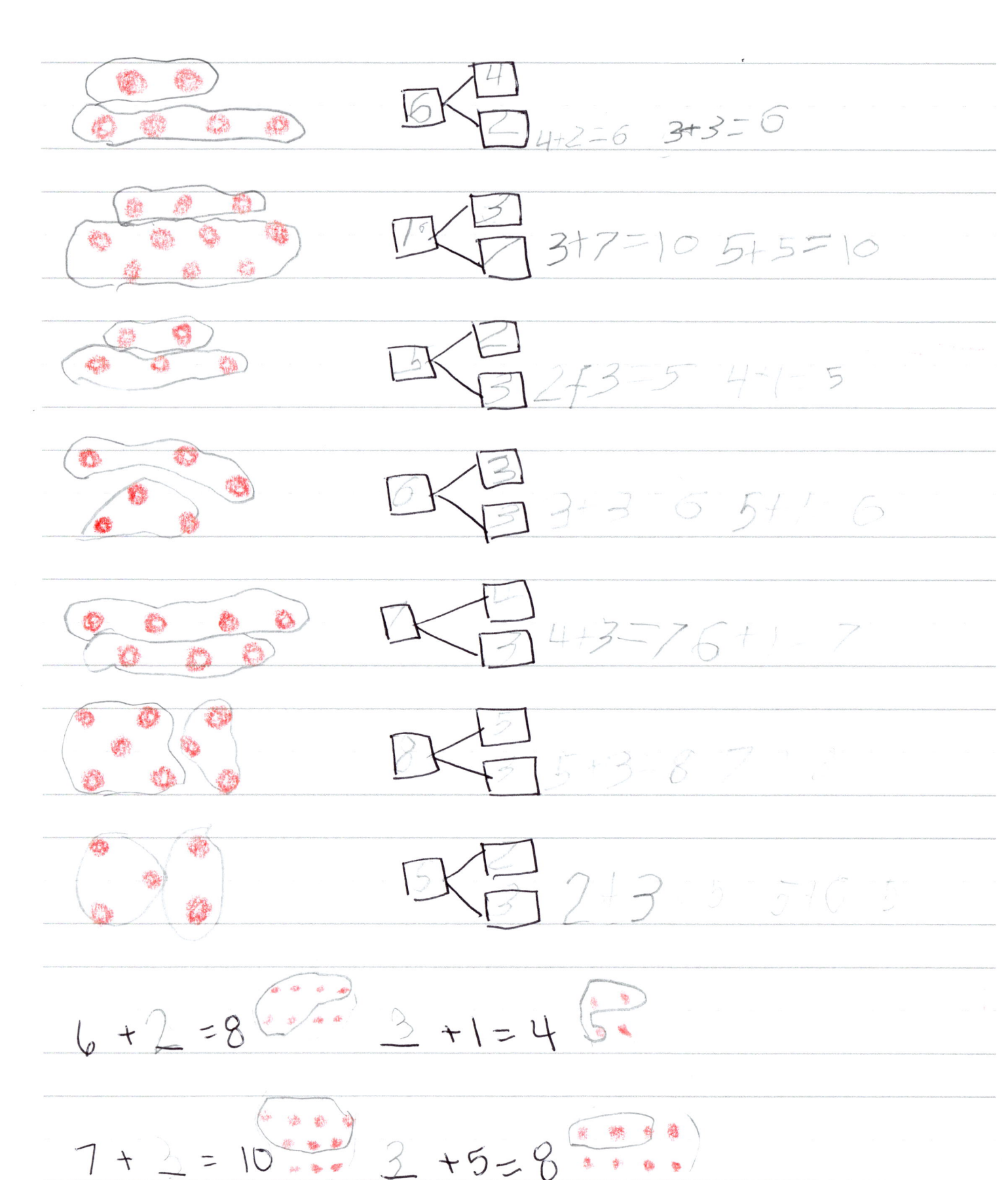

(dots)	6 → 4, 2	4+2=6 3+3=6
(dots)	10 → 3, 7	3+7=10 5+5=10
(dots)	5 → 2, 3	2+3=5 4+1=5
(dots)	6 → 3, 3	3+3=6 5+1=6
(dots)	7 → 4, 3	4+3=7 6+1=7
(dots)	8 → 5, 3	5+3=8 7+1=8
(dots)	5 → 2, 3	2+3=5 5+0=5

6 + 2 = 8   3 + 1 = 4

7 + 3 = 10   3 + 5 = 8

6 + 3 = 9   9 + 3 = 12

and as it pan rich

find if him an spin

for in is now

just is sip cat

many it fit

one pin

she

then

her are	big	in	pin
biy buy	ran	pig	
little	sit	did	
so	did	s	si
Too	its	dig	
p		big	ship
			fun
you			

drip	Try	run
Trap	branch	swim
	end of spelling words	
drum	agin	walk
Trip	away	sleep
gil	becuse	clime
scrub	club	eat
flap	fall	dance
clap	foll	Jump
sled	or	write
club	pritiy	play

thing   blue
think   clue
long   true
thank

pitch
pitches
cent
cents
catch
catches

	-at	-it
I	Bat	Bit
and	Cat	Lit
am	Mat	Mit
like	Fat	sit
see	Pat	hit
Can	cat	Pit
	sat	Kit

Made in the USA
Las Vegas, NV
11 September 2023